Cannonball with feathers

Caroline Carver

Oversteps Books

First published in 2022 by Oversteps Books Ltd
6 Halwell House
South Pool
Nr Kingsbridge
Devon
TQ7 2RX
UK

www.overstepsbooks.com

Copyright © 2022 Caroline Carver
ISBN 978-1-906856-94-6

All rights reserved. No part of this book may be reproduced, stored in a retrieval system, or transmitted in any form, or by any means, electronic, mechanical, photocopying, recording or otherwise, or translated into any language, without prior written permission from Oversteps Books, except by a reviewer who may quote brief passages in a review.

The right of Caroline Carver to be identified as the author of this work has been asserted by her in accordance with the Copyright, Designs and Patents Act 1988.

Printed in Great Britain by imprint digital, Devon

dedicated to
my wonderful husband and family
Michael   Ben   Magda   Daria

and

remembering my mother, a naval wife
my father, a gunnery officer

the view was so beautiful we decided to play the gramophone
my mother wrote on the back of this photo as they looked
down to Lake Wairarapa, the North Island, New Zealand

Acknowledgements

Some of these poems have been published in Acumen, HQ Quarterly, Quadrant, Artemis, Orbis among others, as well as several online sites and non-poetry publications. They've been read by people as far afield as the Arctic exploration team of Parks Canada and muskox farmers in Alaska. Many are translated into Romanian.

I owe special thanks to many: Gabriel Griffin of *Poetry on the Lake* in Orta, Professor Lidia Vianu in Bucharest, Anne Stewart of *poetry pf* in Orpington. I'm grateful to 'Le Mouliners', to FPG friends, especially Penelope Shuttle and Gary Matthews, to D M Thomas and Stray Dogs, to Alwyn Marriage for taking me on a second time, to Susi Clare for her editing eye, and Hilary Elfick for advice on New Zealand. Much thanks to the *Poetry Society*, and to Dilys Wood at *Second Light*.

Thanks for illustrations to: Norman Lister, Jan Robson, Terri Waters Photography and Design. Cover illustration courtesy of Doug Aitken, NEW ERA, 2018. Installation view from Tomorrow is the Question, 2019, ARoS, Denmark. Photo: Anders Sune Berg. Courtesy of ARoS Museum

Most of all, I thank Jamaica, its voice, its joy, its wonderful people. Anyone who lives on the island becomes part of the soil, part of the rock, part of the rainforest, part of of nights filled with the voices of tree-frogs, of blundering moths, excitable fireflies, flowers pushing out bursts of scent. There are duppies. Night swimmers are bathed in phosphorescence – angel-light. Jamaica celebrates the oceans in a still-blue world, binds a child to our planet for life.

Contents

I was a child who loved parrots	1
Bermuda in aspic	2
Letter to my father	3
the sunken trimaran	4
Crossing the Minch	5
my life as a daughter in 44 lines	6
Hurricane Mama	7
Norway Søster poems: birthday	8
Jamaica night	9
Luke	10
Fife	11
what is a husband?	12
the waterfall	13
London Underground	14
swimming with sharks	15
Norway Søster poems: thunder	16
comme çi comme ça	17
Edmonton disconnect	18
fire road cutting	19
Norval spring ice	20
cannonball with feathers	21
Norway Søster poems: turning point	22
turning aside	23
muskox	24
St. Elias Mountains Yukon Territory	25
love in a South Dakota forest	26
panick	27
when you come	28
Puddle	29
Russian market: Warsaw	30
Norway	31
Song of the Ash Tree	32
Kirkenes	33
beyond the forest	34
avocat	35
Bucharest	36

Norway soster poems: from the armchair of happiness	37
la cloche qui sonne	38
bye bye baby	39
Norway Søster poems: sharing	40
Swan song from the Millpond	41
the moving of feet	42
Copenhagen	44
self-puff	45
Norway Søster poem: leaving home	46
Talking to Alice	47
limpet	50
tomorrow is the question	51

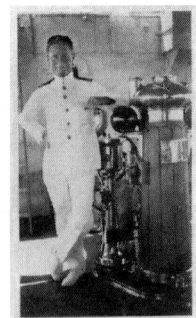

I was a child who loved parrots

everything my mother ate and drank
passed on to me   as I lay curled inside her
still only the size of a small bat
comforted by darkness

I like to think I can remember
the days she soothed us both
as we lay in the waters of a hot spring meadow
listening to cows all round us
pulling on cool grass
that would be translated into milk
into the first sinews and nerves of my body
till I was bound so tight into the landscape
she swears I was born with a stamp on my forehead
made in New Zealand

my mother loved to tell
how southern sun poured down on her
how one day she forgot to turn
the sign on the wicker gate
to read OCCUPIED
and a stranger came
lay beside her in the hot spring water
told her that clouds
floating up from the horizon
were snow babies   born in southern mountains
told her the birds of the islands would bless her child
the kakapo   the yellow and red-crowned
and orange-fronted parakeets
the kiwi   the bellbird   even the long dead moa

Bermuda in aspic

our convoy had already sailed through war
attacked by U-boats mid-Atlantic
we watched the ship behind us as it sank
stern first   the way they do in picture books

a cannonball thundered across our bow
as we neared Bermuda's Citadel
I buried my head in my mother's lap
and this was the first time the tinnitus came to me

Bermuda was still dreaming of its colonial past
men firing cannons from castle battlements

Letter to my father

not the one lying by the whale's mouth
or the one put to sleep in the long drawer
pennies on its eyes
it wasn't found by starlight
when the milky way was so clear
I saw creatures dancing like escaped fauns

no it was you   my father

we shared this world together only a short time
but you showed me how to hold a bluetit
turn it on its back
stroke the soft underside
till it lay calm   first in your hand
and then in my small grasp
my round well-padded fingers

we walked those woods so many afternoons
you talked of all the birds
which moved so fast   I never saw them

the sunken trimaran

my father had his pipe in his mouth
when he dived underwater
swan through the main cabin
to collect the ship's papers
which were floating everywhere

it was still lit when he came up again

sometimes I dispute this story   ask myself
how important is truth?   though maybe
it rounds out the picture of a man long gone
who helped me negotiate overfalls   whirlpools
find my way through the Raz de Sein

have you noticed the pulling sound of water
as it sloshes among rocks
how it sounds like the sucking of a pipe?

the Raz de Sein is a perilous tidal race off Finistère

Crossing the Minch

there was the night I disappeared
into dreams from an old book
heavy with the weight of water on it

my arm attached to an ancient door
set into the walls of a castle
a home for the moon sailing over us
through a skyful of stars

I was no good at the helm   I realised
as I woke with a start   the tiller
still under my arm
and a strange fortress ahead
where no fortress should be
not floating upside down like a mirage
but settled on the horizon

all that night the sea was full of sighs
and the singing and breathing of whales

my life as a daughter in 44 lines

on the doorstep of my life
I left two unpublished novels
The postman needed something
better to deliver than Sears catalogues
I left six plants lined up like dead rats
waiting for badgers to take them away
left the story of my embarrassing encounter
with a stockbroker and his rolled umbrella
who took me to a pub lit by candles
which all blew out as we went in
leaving a lot of angry customers in the dark
I laughed so hard he made me walk home
but my mother said *serve you right and you look
like something the cat brought in* and she said
send that underwear to someone you don't like

would you say I was unlucky with men?
I climbed a mountain with an Austrian guide
and only just made it down again
stole a wallet from a used car salesman
drove myself home in his car leaving him
in the expensive restaurant where he'd taken me
and he had to stay and do the washing up
before hitching 60 miles back to Toronto
it turned out he was proud of my audacity
stalked me when I finally took up
with someone else so now
I'm writing this to my mother
who never knew what to do with me
after my father died for you my mother
I leave the hairbrush you beat me with
without saying what I'd done wrong
until I thought I must be adopted or you'd wanted a son
I return the family christening robe
that's come down through the generations
return the car with its smashed-in fender
the one that rolled down the hill
though no one was killed
and at last I weep for you my mother
as I look at a photograph
of the day you put me on the donkey
walked limping beside me under hot sun
carrying all the shopping bags –
I still sense the unbreakable mother daughter bond
am ashamed of all the pain I put you through

Hurricane Mama

Saba   I going crash through window with eyes wide open
speak with mouth full   of fire water soot
smear pig dirt on nice clean walls you just painted
take my clothes off   my grubby grubby clothes
roll in mud puddles the rain do bring
speak like cowgirl   like possessor of bodies
speak with dun language   foul language
chicken language   heads cut off language
Saba   if they cut my head off   I still keep running

      why you try calm me down?
      why you speak nice when I rage like Hurricane Mama?
      why you no angry?

I hit my head on floor   you still speak to me
I cut my arm   you still speak to me
I cut tablecloth   curtain   counterpane
you still speak to me

no one can fill hole in my head
cure sun-ripped hands
no one can bring my father back to me

but I have memories   you say
is true   I have memories
    will   always
the times he threw me in the air
that is a memory
when he smoked his pipe in evenings
that is a memory
when we walked on beach and he said
*say damn   daughter mine   say dam*n
that is a memory
when he laughed so hard todies and finches flew out of him
that is a memory

I will not cry any more
I will be quiet as moon shining on water
moon making long welcome road over water
I will tell my mind   go after moon on water

bring me water   Saba
after I walk the moon road   I will sleep

'todies' are small and colourful Jamaican birds

7

Norway Søster poems: birthday

søster why are you still awake
when trees cast no shadow
and the moon has scarcely
begun to creep out of her nest?

today was your birthday
you sang when we got up
said we must count everything
we love about our mother
especially the festive birthday lunch
she'd promised us   I could see
you were dreaming about presents
plentiful as seed moths
fluttering in at the window
we watched as mamma went out
gathered up one of the hens
tucking it under her arm as if she cared for it
before pulling its head
away from its neck   we heard the popping sound
even from where we stood
safe in the house   fire blazing with newly-
gathered pine-cones   the forest raging
in early morning light

its legs went on moving   you said
the way mine twitch in the evenings
and I thought of its scattered seed moth mind
longing to get back to the yard
where we'd put down fresh hay
only that morning   where her sisters
still calmly poked about in lifelong sunshine

Jamaica night

I used to think stars were holes
punched in a black arc of curtain
to let in the light behind
so we could shine our own way down dark paths
and on nights when the moon came
it was only a mirror   a reflection
of earth-light returned to us
glittering on the river as it slid
its way among trees   a few leaves floating on it
and I would feel comforted

but now I've learned about planets and satellite
moons   how the universe is expanding
each time I look up at the stars   they seem further away
and I open my mind to this but all I can feel
is a strange loneliness   because one day
the comfort of lights may be gone

I used to think the voices of whistling frogs at night
was the sound of stars twinkling
and all seemed to very right with the world
I'm not yet allowing my mind to tread
the stony path of quantum physics
or to think   even for a minute
that every time I raise a glass to the future
or consider something that happened today
there may be a thousand identical me's in other places
doing the same thing
our cottage with its comforting cob walls and pictures
and rooms leading into other rooms
may be stepping away from me
and like the planets and universes
moving backwards and further away
until there is no more centre to my life
no warm comfort
no more goldfinches in the garden
nowhere where I can hide myself and feel
this is my safe place   this is my home

Luke

a small breeze
sets the vanes in motion
till they creak like angry parrots
but there you are
the dare's been accepted
Luke
the easiest to bully
is going to set us right

we watch his shaking knees
as he moves slowly
rung by rusted rung
up to the top
early manhood
even at eight
falling suddenly upon him

it only takes one rusted rung to break

perhaps this
never happened
perhaps five terrified children
never saw
a boy called Luke
fall from the water tower

never saw his body
splayed out on its concrete base

because this happened far from my home
and none of the grown-ups
ever talked about it

Fife
5 March 1978

after the hospital called
to say my mother had died
I went to the beach
looked across the Firth
all the water in it   fresh from the sea

I took off my shoes
it was winter   but I needed to curl my toes
into cold shell-crushed sand
I needed to touch something
so I could understand my history

what is a husband?

someone who is courteous and kind, who never forgets
how to be this

*except during arguments, slammed doors,
stamping out of rooms (me, that is)*

who always has to be reminded of birthdays, anniversaries,
things not important in the Great Scheme of Things

someone who cleans up after the cat's been sick again
without fussing

insists on doing the washing up, peels potatoes
and hulls strawberries

who is one of the best dads ever
whose heart is larger than anyone's

but still after half a century together, intensely private
who is very fond of the dog *(and the dog of him)*

who puts up with the cat because she was found
as a half-dead orphan

someone I never write about because our world
is set in a dark forest

full of our own private trails, solitudes, joys
and near-disasters

the waterfall

not Raymond Carver's
not Wordsworth's or Walt Whitman's
nor any of the Naiad-rich
fantasies of Greek mythology

my waterfall is mine   travels with me
in its sealed-tight DIPLOMATIC BAG
that says. Don't touch
I lock it with my special golden key
guarded by passwords I can change each day

sometimes when I travel with my waterfall
it says *let's go back to the house*
without walls
we'll stand in the shower room
you and me   says the waterfall
you must put your back to the tiles
facing into the breeze of a stone-walled garden
no one can see us so
reach up and turn me on baby
reach up and turn me on

London Underground

here under the ground says the teacher
under this soft stubby grass
under all the weevils and kill-you-off spiders
under the silent worms millions of microbes
yes look down   you must try and imagine
tunnels passageways creaking elevators
imagine humans like ants there are so many
all crowding down with their faraway faces
if you can imagine this   girls
you will know what it's like to live in London

we Jamaicans gaze down at the grass   its multitude
of life forms   its kindness to feet
think down to the limestone heart of the island
the caves and grottos   fish   electric eels
and we cannot imagine tunnels and trains
replacing the glitter of stalactites   gentle curves
made by millennia of soft sea fingers
soothing these walls into water palaces

sun beats down on our heads

we think the London Underground
should have boats   fishermen
heavy-voiced frigate birds
not the trains' *diddy dum* as they move into stations
where brakes   you say   sound like abandoned gulls
as pads check   wheels sigh   cling to the tracks
until the doors open   throw people out
suck people in

we decide we will not go to London

swimming with sharks

I once swam with sharks
in the Bahamas
graceful   indifferent   dangerous

fingered sea anemones
languid as the dancers
my father loved to watch in Tongatapu

at school we'd dissected a shark
in our laboratory
stroked it   till its knife-edged skin
drew blood from our fingers

took it in turns to swing
her amniotic sac from side to side
making three perfect embryos
move slowly up and down

I still remember the sight of them
shining against the light
wish we hadn't stopped them
being born

Norway Søster poems: thunder

søster I can predict   I can swear on mountains
I can count maidens
because I know
when you arrive with a face like that
it doesn't matter that I am getting out the special cloth
spreading it   so no creases remain
laying the plates just right   choosing the mugs
that usually bring a smile to your face   today
nothing will take the crimp out of your lips
not the sunshine   day-and-night sun
not the bright geraniums
I've planted outside your window
not our lilac   hanging onto its blooms
nor bees that have come from nowhere
to brighten our lives
disease is wiping them out you say
and I know   when you look across to the islands
you see   not beaches   not clear water
where only yesterday we swam
but jagged mountains   crouched like lions
at the edge of the sea
Vikings   swarming down to the boats   cries
not from gulls   but wailing women and children

comme çi comme ça

why didn't we pay a bit more and have a view?
I was asking   when there was a thud
as a small migrating finch hit the glass windows
and fell on its back as if dead

reminding me of my first day in this new country   Canada
when our train jerked to a halt in the middle of a forest
and the conductor came through in his smart uniform
shrugging and saying   *life's always comme çi comme ça*
he spread his hands wide to show the gaps in life
someone's just been killed at the level crossing he said
and now many years later we are in a western railway town
where the guidebook struggles to find excitement
and a bird has flown into that same small space
where life drops out of one world and into another

they say *He cares for every sparrow that falls*
I imagine Him up there shaking his head
saying *c'est toujours comme çi comme ça*
this is the way it is   but sometimes   kindness creeps in
and when we open the window the finch is stirring
I pick it up as my father taught me
stroke its breast as it lies motionless in my hand
till it turns its head to look sideways at me
springs into the air   flies away

later we eat outside at one of the tables
looking out at the lake   study a flock of birds
under our feet   hope our finch is among them
enjoying crumbs dropped by our fellow travellers
hoping this thought is a true one

Edmonton disconnect
for Jean   whose story it is

there's a slight *what if?* tremor that comes
when you walk arm in arm with a boy from your class
the new boy   hair falling over his face
how much can he see?   there's no moon
somehow trees are making it darker than usual
but you have to get home   and your mother said
don't ever go in the park on your own again
so you've asked him to walk with you
shift your pack slightly   wonder whether
when there's no light   people   start communicating
in ways beyond words like a slight squeeze on the arm
but you don't want to make conversation
because what happened in this park three days ago
is still raw   the papers full of pictures of the girl
of the place where a jogger saw a naked foot
sticking out from the bushes   and now you can't think

of anything else   you're right where they found her
*do the police rake the ground over once the clean-up's done
or is that dark patch blood?* perhaps the boy feels the same
his arm trembles   maybe he too is afraid   but at last
you get to the road with its comforting streetlamps
thank him   he doesn't want to go   as if
a special bond holds you together   but you head home
tell your parents how kind he was   polite   a bit old-fashioned
you say you didn't talk   but something special passed
between you   a kind of warm non-language thing
like the way animals message each other   *you'd like him*
you tell them   so at first you can't believe it when the police come
show you photographs   ask you to identify him

fire road cutting
north of the 60th parallel

people say it's too cold to snow
but when I set off at midday   snow was falling

I waited for you so long my love   but you did not come

dark seemed early creeping through trees
like a visitation of black-cloaked women
so I bivouac'd beside the cut digging a hollow
lining it with branches   as you've taught me
I know you'd be proud of the way I've set my fire
see how it leaps and claps its hands
see how carefully I've placed it
away from overladen branches

now I'm your frugal housewife again
heating snow to make a pot of tea

the Northern Lights were early tonight
hesitant at first   tiptoeing onto the skyline
soon they'll be confident enough to dance for both of us
everything will shine green and red and mauve
add diamonds to my cheeks

you haven't asked how I am   cold is the answer
it sinks into my bones   until even marrow congeals
I'll keep the fire burning tonight
and I won't falter   I know I'm not alone
elk and wolves surround me   and I found
blood on the snow   signs of a scuffle
prints of frightened snowshoe rabbits

how quiet it is!   nothing between us and the North Pole
except this silent boreal forest
with its guardian angels in coronets of green

I've waited for you so long   my love   but you have not come

Norval spring ice
Ontario

the ice went out of the river like a bullying giant
destroying a playground   that till now
had been the peaceful frozen face of water
with children skating   ducks trying to walk on it

the ice broke up in angry complaint
you could hear it coming two bends away
hear its clattering voice   the way
the river was tossing every toy out of itself
before it roared into sight
gigantic untidiness borne in its brawny arms
tray-loads of ice stacked on top of each other

the ice and the river came into sight
snatching at grass and weeds
snapping small branches   pulling down trees
came into sight like a deposed emperor
last winter's trophies piled up so high
it stuck under the footbridge
ice-melt spring water building behind it
and flooding the surrounding fields

we climbed a small hill and watched
as it finally managed to force
the bridge away from its roots   how proudly
it bore it downriver   like a dog with a dinosaur bone
two sets of steps trailing limply behind it

cannonball with feathers

I flew like a grouse bursting from cover
I flew like the spangled lady fired from a gun
to the top of the circus tent   only here on the snow
there seems no limit to how high I can go
as my skis climb an unexpected mogul
and I soar out over the main slope
hoping I won't land on an innocent child
or a tough old lady meandering downhill

for a few glorious moments I hover
I fly   looking down on a sparkling slope
its happy people   and fall in love again
with the transforming power of snow
the way it lies on branches   plays
with balance and gravity   I think of Galileo
his feather   the tower of Pisa   wonder
what my husband will make of me
taking to the sky like this   while our son
continues downhill alone on his short child skis

and suddenly I've landed
but still I fly on   landbound but upright
dreaming of hot chocolate   Strauss
skaters waltzing on a forest pond
remember I once skied over a small precipice
and was saved by a tree where I hung
upside down till a handsome man rescued me
and now   as then   I hear Galileo asking *I mean
how long did you think you could stay up there?*

Norway Søster poems: turning point

søster we are already fighting about which way to go
though when we got up this morning   we agreed harmony
was the basis for a good relationship   and anyway
we are joined at the hip so to speak   having the same mother
and I think same father   living in the same house
eating the same food   unless it's one of those mornings
when you push your plate away asking   *what is this rubbish?*
why do we always have to eat the same thing?
today you seemed happy as our mother packed sandwiches
sent us off   and now we have reached the crossroads
with firm instructions to take the left road into the town
because right leads through the forest and an encampment
of gypsies   but you want to go straight ahead
and down to the sea   suddenly I agree   don't want to fight
for fighting's sake   warmth pours into my body
because this once only we understand each other   even
hold hands   such a strange thing for us to do   carry straight on
perhaps this is what our mother hoped   knowing *'ahead'*
would always hold something different for each of us   for you
islands with their inviting cottages   moored boats nudged
against smart new-build jetties   for me
the ring of skerries beyond   where tingling water
cushions a rocky hinterland of witches and trolls

turning aside

I'm going to start my journey the way Eskimos do
not travelling in a straight line   not planning a route
not trying to keep within footpaths of thought
but opening my mind to the slightest change
in this landscape of unrelenting ice and snow
perhaps it's a touch of wind on my face
that whispers   more cold is coming   or it's a glimpse
of something small   like this ground squirrel
I've zigzagged away to see   we'll sit down together
talk   not with the directness of my people
no   not with words   but quiet fingers of thought
as if he's a shaman   yes   we're in this together
each taking different things from the landscape
for him it's the never-ending search for food
shamrock   lichen   sphagnum moss   or treasure
I know he's partial to socks to line his nest   he
and his brother stole mine while I was sleeping
I bear no grudge   we share the same sweep of vision
our lives converge with the same force
when we're here on top of the world
I look with awe at the unchanging horizon
know my purpose has been strengthened
by stepping aside for a while

muskox
i.m. Barry Lopez 1945 – December 2020

if I were a muskox
I'd think sedges and lichen
I'd moon over them   breathe over them
pull at them with my soft lips
savour bluegrass willowherb
bladderwort campion
foxtail   cowberry
mountain sorrel   Labrador tea
(this last trending on eBay but not common)
when I had eaten I'd caress the ground
with my wise beard
shake long feathery skirts
bury my face in your already thick coat
Murmur *umingmak* to you
umingmak my little poppet calf
its only by knowing one's proper name
one finds one's place in the universe

St Elias Mountains   Yukon Territory

who was king in that year?   or queen   or whatever
you like to name it   I prefer something that suggests
not obsequiousness   toe-licking   leaving rooms backwards
but a   *hey haven't we met before?   remember me
I was one of a thousand hands you shook that day*
okay   I'm falling into the trap again   let's not go
pinning a badge on me   sling a ribbon round my neck
just because on hands and knees   I crawled the last half mile
back to camp   over rock and snow   inch by painful inch

my first official mountain had finished me
(7 miles to the base   3 thousand feet up
crampons on the face   ice-axe in hand)   then down again

graceful and airy   was how I'd felt up there
now I returned to camp on all fours
wondering if the valley grizzly had followed me
please don't eat my feet   I said to him
they were so good to me on the mountain

anxious faces peered from the mess as I crawled in
hands helped me up   gave me the most precious drink
we'd carried in   beer   heavy as rocks
beer   in a triumphal tin mug   beer   the best I ever had
and he-who-led-the-first-ever-successful-Everest-expedition
came and shook my hand   *no need to call me 'sir'*   he said

Canada celebrated its Centenary in 1967, and the Alpine Club saluted this by sending experienced members to climb and name 12 mountains in the Yukon. Amateur climbers like me were allowed to accompany the expedition.

love in a South Dakota forest

our tent was a ship
pitching and tossing
as he clung to the entrance poles
snuffled and sang
of the fish he'd caught
of his longing for cookies   *wieners*
plastic-wrapped hamburgers
anything we might have for him

impatient
he went down on all fours
snuffed his way round
the untethered base of our tent
grunted as he tripped on a guy rope

you see   I was on my left side
facing out   when he stopped
his nose was two inches from my nose
we might have been lovers
poised to kiss   only a scrap
of as yet unblooded cotton
lay between us and consummation

I was saved   only when
the door of a nearby car opened
and he paused   stood up
shambled away   his tread
waking night scents
of pine trees and moss   my breath
still in his body   as his was in mine

all the next day
on our long journey over the Sierra
his memory stayed in my mouth   berried
    musky   with traces of fish   I kept looking back
till we reached the Pacific
turned one last time
wanting to share this moment with him
tell him about whales and bald eagles
ask the best way to catch salmon

panick

a horse may shy   so as not to lose its footing
and the rider will frown as a shiver of muscle
runs over its shoulders where he or she has laid
the reins for a moment   perhaps this rider will learn
what you and I are about to find out
that magic comes when two opposites face each other
when there's a crackle in the air
and you can seize the moment   *carpe diem*
pass your hand through a wind traveller
(one who drifts without purpose or direction)
because the only thing you can be certain of
is that you too are sitting on your horse
reins on its shoulders   looking out to sea
from the top of a cliff where caves wait underneath you
wait for sun to creep through those dark crevices
mixing misfortune with hope   plague with despair
only they hold the key to understanding   forgiving
know the ways into your mind   where words have woken
and are busy again   laying themselves out in patterns
nudging each other as they cross the wind man's space
between dark and light   they were hiding so deep
in your soul   only a poem could gather them in again

when you come

when you come I'll show how life has been without you
when my ship tossed and turned with the wind
with you no longer at the tiller   I'll show how my body
moulds with the years   like a reef slowly growing
up to the surface   taking its time
I'll lie on my side   so the peaks and curves
are sometimes there and sometimes not
because whatever I do   I can't stop the tide
the shush and stir of it   the quiet whispering

all's calm with me now   but there's no hiding
because when a storm comes   it takes
my carefully folded secrets   exposes them
like remnants of a wreck   like a boat
worn back to spars and bone   its beauty eaten away

for many years after you'd gone   when I was landbound
I used to drive through country lanes   watch how they changed
depending on the light   in my mind I would say
here's where we stopped and listened to music
because the view was so beautiful
because when we turn that corner
the sea with all its inlets and bays is suddenly there again
remember how we caught our breath as if we'd never seen it before
brushing against the land   taking pictures of it
playfully making a record of all that's important in our world
only upside down

Puddle

you step into it delicately
as if it's a pool for a naiad
though it's only
a dusty eye in the road
where earth and tarmac hold the fort

your bare feet were itching
to soothe an assault of prickles
pesky flies   a narrow band of sun
they sigh with relief

but you are still trying
as you have all your life
to figure out why
it grabs the heart

perhaps it reminds you
of womb water
or the ocean you came from
don't be silly   say your feet
as they swish around in the water

Russian market: Warsaw

home is where one starts from   Good grief!
if I'd been born here I too might be condemned to serve
on a stall in this sun-baked place
reminding me of a disused movie set

derelict rows of stalls overflow with bounty
Nikon cameras   T-shirts   American jeans   caged chickens
looking as if they came on a starvation march to get here
stray dogs   untrustworthy   sour-faced
phlegmatic thin-flanked cows   even down-at-heel camels

under the awnings   people shelter from the heat
one unexpected couple hold hands
out of necessity?   propping each other up?
where did they start from?   were they happy once
food in their mouths   children dawdling in the playground
asking   must we go home now?
how did these one-time innocents end up here
on a strip of tarmac wide enough to blast a tank through?

further in   you tell me   there are parachute maps
hand grenades   ejector seats   bazookas   balaclavas
bayonets   AK-47s   one can stock up on second-hand warplanes
tear gas   plutonium   enriched uranium   bomb-making kits
oceans of dark glasses   everyone wears them   even me
one can have anything one fancies   even
the buying and selling of children perhaps?
fronted by enough cheap Nikes to shoe Europe

the couple who are not in love   come from behind their stall
walk towards us with the chill stiff-legged alertness
of forest predators   *we better go home*   my son mutters
pulling me away

Norway

the land of the midnight sun
has no pity on strangers
the sun will not go away
leave space for
forgiveness of dark silence
the blue black velvetness of woods
bursting point
for the imagination

dull light hangs heavy
over a grey sea
even the boreal forest has gone

only the barren lands
offer bleak morsels of grass

Song of the Ash Tree

like Yggdrasil the great ash
with her snake coiled at the root
we are bound by water and hope

roots reaching deep into that kingdom
of ferns and wet darkness
where past   present   and future

water each life from the sacred well
Did you know – in those high days of summer
when shadows retreat into the forest –

and the wind rustles our leaves
till we burst with love
male   female   or androgynous

we are always the wild ones of woodland
wrapped in ivy   dancing with Satyrs

Seize the day   pretty child   Seize the day

when you are matronly
bunched keys at your thickening waist
every leaf you grow

every kindness every point of suffering
will be carved into your face
unless you have gazed nightly through shy leaves

dreaming of both water and fire
the milk-soft bloom of stars
lambs in their brief dance of spring

Kirkenes

in this nondescript semi-deserted place
where streets are named in two languages
there's a great art gallery   bookshop

and museum   the usual gambling joint
and a spy ship tied up at the dock

Kirkenes straddles two time-zones
I want to stop and ask someone
how do you know when to get up?

but I don't speak Norwegian or Russian
and the streets are deserted

I have coffee in an outdoor café
empty except for one small boy
chasing a pigeon between tables

it's head   like a double time-zone clock
ticks backwards and forwards

this touch of normality's comforting
I think as I head back to our ship
by way of a deserted no-man's land

where a few determined flowers crack concrete
and a man is carrying a bulging black bag

in our own ship's laundry room
someone sits hiding in one of the cubicles
enormous work-boots show under the door

prisoner? murderer? spy? imagination runs riot
as we close our porthole against 24 hour sun

Kirkenes, almost 70° north, is a small town in Norway
near the Finnish / Russian border

beyond the forest

in the Carpathian Mountains
of Transylvania
you may find bears and wolves
but though I walked there
I never saw one   and no
there are no vampires

so   open this forest book for me
let me live in a house with
low-beamed ceilings   lamp-lit rooms
the magic of fruit-carved armoires
soft-polished wood floorboards
the scent of plum brandy

let me sense the smells of pine and moss
the chink of cowbells   let me wake
in a house with horses outside
their legs so long they can run
to the moon and back in a morning
Let me sleep in a bed full of history

let me meet a count so handsome
I burst into tears when I see him

avocat

The rabbi fitted his burning torch
into a rusted metal holder
wedged in the rough stone wall

there was something about the way
he persevered   prayer shawl slipping
from his shoulders   but he couldn't right it

wax dripped onto the flagstone floor
as he sang the Kaddish
in his reedy wavering voice

afterwards we went outside
stood round the unnervingly deep grave
clutching icy handfuls of earth for the coffin

I felt part of the way of things held by the forest
its trees and branches
caught in wisps of fog

as the Rabbi spoke of our uncle
a cultured man who spoke no English
but learned to do the Times crossword

after a while I stopped listening
because something else was mysteriously
creeping under his voice   his words faltered

as   dreamlike figures
emerged from the trees
violins tucked under their chins

wraiths   freed from some hinterland
between here and the afterlife   shreds
of music floated into the clearing

broke my heart   and we stood   stunned
I told the Rabbi about my uncle's work
with the Roma   his life-long help for them

I must go and thank them   he said
invite them for a glass of Țuică
but they had paid their tributes and gone

Bucharest

the park was full of trees
with black trunks and black branches
reminding me of paintings by an artist
whose name I couldn't remember
my mind jumped out of my body
and went running among them
asking each one *what are you trying to say to me?*
and this took a long time there were so many
but I couldn't stop
or leave any of them out because the eye of the artist
had directed me to look at all of them carefully
until finally I understood that language
on its own doesn't matter because
it's becoming an outdated way of communication
and I must remember that time runs backwards
as well as forwards   so I looked
with all the strength of my eyes
and though I could now hear voices behind me
I didn't want to turn or hear what they were saying
I didn't want to be told we live in a failing world

Norway Søster poems: from the armchair of happiness

when we run down through deep pasture
where my head starts to feel like a balloon
because I'm happy and I don't know where
to store my thoughts   save them for later
they buzz and twinkle at me   *now now now*
and here's the river waiting for us at the bottom
sounding like the old hen it is
singing and chuckling its way through and over
what to me might be life-threatening obstacles
of smoothed and rounded pebbles and stones
but to the water are only good adventures in a cheery life
it's always at this point that I turn and see
your scowling face lagging behind me
feel that dull thud in my shrinking balloon
like the sound they say was made
when two black holes bumped into
and demolished each other 7 billion years ago
and we've only just heard it

like them we are fighters in a ring so huge
my bubble of happiness pops and vanishes
but today I am strong   ignore you
settle on a low rock by the river
reach in for a stone far enough away from the main current
to preserve a slight hint of moss
perhaps it's getting ready to settle down
take life as it is   my only problem
as a stone lover
is to choose between so many
which one will be my favourite today

la cloche qui sonne

it wasn't the serenity of Tollund Man   or the heart-stopping
Mesolithic remains of a baby put to rest in a swan's wing
it wasn't the harmony of unaccompanied medieval voices
singing Spem in Alium *a song of fortie partes made by Mr Tallys*
or a sea where phosphorescence coated my body with light
it was that evening in France when we returned to the waiting house
and were reunited with our teenage son   I woke at 3 gazing up
through the high circular window at a sky overflowing with stars
heard a cock crow   followed by   from across the valley
the ancient monastery bell tolling its single *yin* and *yang* note
in an old man's voice   echoing back to ancient China and filled
with miracles   sometimes it was rung at times of war or disaster
but tonight all I could hear was each note hanging on the air
telling of hope   wonder and that delicate luminous word *love*

bye bye baby

the woman takes her baby down to the beach
Sea   if you are watching   notice how she holds it
like the newborn it is   she wants you to take it in your arms
sing it a lullaby   she wants her baby to be as happy as sandflies
on a hot day   dancing with all their multitudes of family
she wants her baby to learn the magic of oceans
the inevitability of water   she wants it to know how to hold back
at the right time and move forward at others
wants it to feel crushed shells under its fingers
and the heavy pull as sea draws back again
the woman wants her child to be able to wait
in the mornings   in the secret place where waves also wait
she wants it to race towards its destiny
feel that magnetic pull of tides against its skin
until it must lie down to avoid the full force
of the *saltstraumen*   she wants it to understand subtleties
of invisible currents   moist winds blowing from the land
in the evening time   she wants her baby's body to be just like you
strong   independent   and all of a whole
under the late-night moon   when sea seems as solid
as sheets of ice   cracking and rubbing
their edges together   in a way that reminds her of something
she can't quite bring herself to think about

Norway Søster poems: sharing

you are not good at loving   *søster*
sometimes you think I'm not looking
and I see it in your face
the way you watch our mother as you take
the last *julekake*   pour *aquavit*
for yourself only   it doesn't matter
she always looks at you with tenderness
she never shows to me
perhaps that's what mothers do
prefer the ones they must work hardest for

Swan song from the Millpond

Pssssssssst they sang every morning as they cam<u>e</u> in
stately and beautiful as always
and as clean as if they'd spent the night
at the launderette   they looked like
the kind of swans you'd want to strike up
a friendship with   share a crumb or two
remembering the day others came and knocked
on the side of our boat   so polite   *hem hem* they said
*good mornin*g we said   and gave them most
of our breakfast   because that was in Scotland
and the Sabbath   and the shop was shut
so it was a fearful shock when   back in Cornwall
we learned at the Mill the cob was singing *shut the duck up!*
as he shooed those dear quacking creatures
away from what he thought of as His pond

but then   as he prepared to sail away
for the last time   he dipped his elegant long neck
into the water   collected some eel grass wrapped in a poem
and laid it on the bank as an offering
to friends present and past   *will you miss us?* he asked

the moving of feet

there's a Scottish island between two islands
where herdsmen take their cattle
for summer grazing   but cows are not good swimmers
they must be loaded into boats
four cows to a boat   believe me
this is not as easy as it sounds
it takes most of one day and at least two men
to persuade a sceptical cow
to step into a boat
one man to make her go
one man to see
she doesn't put her foot through it

reindeer are also moved to summer pasture
but they allow themselves
to be persuaded into the water
heck   they are good swimmers
and northern seas have no crocodiles

there's a river in Africa where animals
listen freely to Nature
every spring   it tells the wildebeest
there's good grass on the other side of the river
it will fill your bellies with joy
make your calves big and strong like you

these messages come like a bolt from the sky
the gods themselves are speaking to them
earth shakes with their thundering hooves
as they crash downhill to the river
me too   me too   they shout
as they hurtle down to the river

oh dear

these voices are also speaking
to crocodiles in the river
telling them good breakfasts and lunches
are hurrying down to the river
everywhere in the world

good breakfasts and lunches are running
down to rivers and grasslands
pronghorns are running
cheetahs and bison are running
rabbits with cute escutcheons are running
lemmings are falling over cliffs
in a mad parody of running

pigs and wild boar are flying from their oppressors
white horses and black bulls of the Camargue are running
hooves drumming on the sandy-ness of almost water
road-runners and ostriches and rheas are running
mice are running   rats are climbing hawsers of ships
ducks are running   on water
jesus lizards are running even faster on water

and we too are running   in our slow clumsy way
please help   mr president   god   whoever it is
who keeps us running
fleeing hiding stumbling along
our lives in bundles on our backs
our children limping behind us
our feet have always been running   walking
hoping for heaven   only a hop and a skip away
in those sweet grasslands on the other side
where calves and children play and grow
where there's enough food for everyone
where no one ever meets a crocodile

Copenhagen

the little mermaid sits sleepless on her rock
longing to return to the sea
though here in our all-in-one airbnb
our son has drifted into
the contented lands of *hygge*

streetlight shows his face returning
from middle life to childhood
as the mind   untethered
slips its moorings   voyages
into night's mysterious moonlit world

self-puff

when you put brown paper bag on head
breathe in and out
paper go away   come back   go   come back
make cave in place where mouth should be
that is self-puff

when you lie in boat   small boat   on your back
look up at darkness   easy cloud   star maidens
run your hand over side   pull shining alchemy
from water   your mouth small *o* of pleasure
that is self-puff

when moon lie upside down on sand
shine through glow-water
back and forth trembling   of glow-water
when you hug yourself because you make sea magic
that is self-puff

when wisps of thought shape themselves on bow
and those wisps are you   only you
that is self-puff *magnifico*

Norway Søster poem: leaving home

there was the day you left home for the first time
we stood on the bridge that ran over the stream
which we'd always pretended was important
a bridge for a prince to use   if one came our way
but sometimes we ran fast down the hillside
gathered ourselves   jumped across
or we swung on the rope   *you tarzan   me jane*
letting go just before the end of the trajectory
so we could grasp the scruff of bank   you laughed
if I fell in   I hated you for doing everything better
for knowing how to please people
that's the interesting one   they'd nod to each other
but I was the one with sharp ears
and now you were going
I cried myself into hiccupping semi-silence
looked at our parents   saw the bits of them
repeated in you   never in myself
I was afraid   without you
I would disappear into sun-sheltering woods
and though people would hunt me for a long time
call out sniffer dogs   beaters would square the fields
the hens droop   stop laying   no one would ever find me

Talking to Alice

Alice
hunched like a hedgehog
blows us a kiss
from her cupped hand

holds it out
perhaps to be shaken
to ask for help
to wave at someone

this hand has endured
more hardship
than is written
in the whole of my vocabulary

even the smallest finger
is filled with courage

sometimes   Alice
you veer to the left

one hand trails the wall
a leg splays out

don't favour your right side
your mother must have said

guilt spilling from her mouth
like milk not offered

I picture a child
at one end of a seesaw

someone comes
stamps on the other end

even the slightest shift
can change everything

continued/

I watch you limp
through city crowds
it's a slow business

you know everyone
and friendship's
no small matter

in one of your dreams
you tell me
you rise from the sea
tall and glittering
in a cloak of stars
like a new-born naiad

Alice   I want to tell you about *Torghatten*
the mountain with a hole in it

it may have been made
by the arrow of a troll

the troll may have been spurned
by a beautiful maiden

the arrow may have pierced rock
left a hole in the shape of a hat

or the hat may have been thrown
by a magician who saved maidens

night may still be hiding under our feet
but one thing's certain

if we step through this hole
the sun will be shining

today you're searching the park
quartering it   looking for
scraps of paper to write on

a harvest moon
has put poetry into your mind
I know the bag you carry
is filled with the stubs of pencils

life's a lottery   isn't it Alice
which of us gets entitlement
inherits the big house   the fast car

I'd rather have the lesser deal
bit of a struggle
chance to work things out for myself

I have to say
I wouldn't have the strength
to survive as you do
you've shown me a thing or two
I won't forget that

on my last night I sat on the pavement
with my book and my dog and a blanket
a stranger had given me

and I sang of the river with its quiet voice
of the day I found white violets
crushed under leaves

I sang of trees in the park
the way they care for each other
reach out through their long roots

and I asked them to keep you safe   Alice
keep you dry when it rains
give you warmth when you lean against them

tears ran down my face as you waved
when I watched your small figure disappear
into the detritus of the city

if one day you're not there anymore
if you never come back
how will I know who to ask
where I can find you?

limpet

did you know   asks the limpet
I have the strongest tongue of all creatures?
I could use a few handholds like you   I say
as I struggled up what's become a vertical precipice
I wonder why I go on   except I believe
rock is the life-saving marrow of the world

I have this vision of *far below*
a place where   hiding among deep aquifers
there are Xanadu caverns   worlds of ice
lakes   animals   perhaps even small trees
people being kind to each other
you're dreaming says the limpet
and he falls off with a sigh
like soft waves shushing back from the shore

soon my soul and yours and maybe his as well
if he has one   will hang in the sky
among a zillion trillion other stars
guardians of a too bright summer moon
and beside me   a polar bear asleep
her paws tingling and twitching
as she remembers
the special feel of a frozen sea
remembers motherhood
the once beautiful white fur of her cubs
lying dead on what's left of the ice

please tell me this is only a dream
I say to the limpet
forgetting he's no longer here

tomorrow is the question
i morgen er spørgsmålet

gone –
timepieces
atomic clocks
rusted satellite dishes
too old for the game

no-one left to ponder
mathematical equations
count seasons of the moon
predict the next eclipse
or touch each other

the universe will continue
on its own stately cycles
without Hamlet   Pythagoras   Da Vinci

earth will turn blue again
for other eyes

unless we change   you say
unless there's still time to change

Oversteps Books Ltd

The Oversteps list includes books by the following poets:

Jean Atkin, R V Bailey, Michael Bayley, Charles Bennett, Denise Bennett, Rebecca Bilkau, Patricia Bishop, Anne Born, Sue Boyle, Melanie Branton, David Broadbridge, Avril Bruton, Maggie Butt, Caroline Carver, Ian Royce Chamberlain, A C Clarke, Ross Cogan, James Cole, Robert Cole, Chris Considine, Christopher Cook, Rose Cook, John Daniel, Miriam Darlington, Will Daunt, Sue Davies, Carol DeVaughn, Hilary Elfick, Jan Farquarson, Sally Festing, Rose Flint, Rebecca Gethin, Terry Gifford, Giles Goodland, Cora Greenhill, David Grubb, Charles Hadfield, Oz Hardwick, Jan Harris, Ken Head, Bill Headdon, Graham High, Jenny Hockey, Jenny Hope, Doris Hulme, Susan Jordan, Ann Kelley, Helen Kitson, Wendy Klein, Kathleen Kummer, Marianne Larsen, Patricia Leighton, Genista Lewes, Anne Lewis-Smith, Dana Littlepage Smith, Janet Loverseed, Mary Maher, Antony Mair, Alwyn Marriage, Marie Marshall, Fokkina McDonnell, Joan McGavin, Denise McSheehy, Andrew Nightingale, Christopher North, David Olsen, Jennie Osborne, Helen Overell, Mandy Pannett, Melanie Penycate, W H Petty, Glen Phillips, Sue Proffitt, Simon Richey, Lynn Roberts, Mary Robinson, Elisabeth Rowe, Ron Scowcroft, Ann Segrave, Richard Skinner, Alex Smith, Jane Spiro, Robert Stein, Anne Stewart, Angela Stoner, John Stuart, Paul Surman, Michael Swan, Diane Tang, Susan Taylor, Michael Thomas, John Torrance, Mark Totterdell, James Turner, Anthony Watts, Christine Whittemore and Simon Williams.

For details of all these books, information about Oversteps and up-to-date news, please look at our website and blog:

www.overstepsbooks.com
http://overstepsbooks.wordpress